Tomorrow's Alphabet

By
George Shannon
Pictures by
Donald Crews

SCHOLASTIC INC.
New York Toronto London Auckland Sydney

Watercolors were used for the full-color art.
The text type is Akzidenz Grotesk.

ISBN 0-590-12709-8

12 11 10 9 8 7 6 5 4 3 2 1   7 8 9/9 0 1 2/0

Printed in the U.S.A.   09
First Scholastic printing, September 1997

For Brian, Andrew, and
Kaitlyn Shannon
–G. S.

For Ann, Nina, and Amy,
and the Gang at Greenwillow
and Susan and Ava (who put her foot in it)
–D. C.

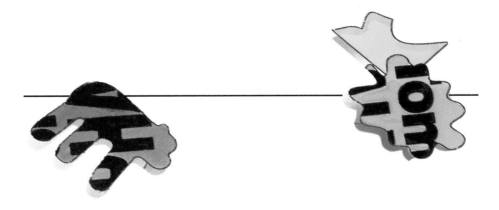

A is for seed–

tomorrow's

APPLE

B
is for eggs–

tomorrow's

BIRDS

c is for milk–

D is for puppy—

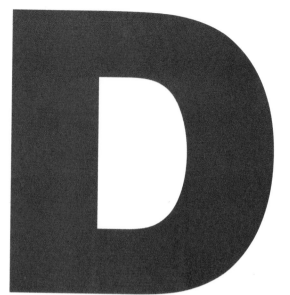

tomorrow's

DOG

E is for campfire–

tomorrow's

EMBERS

F  is for wheat–

tomorrow's

FLOUR

is for
bulbs–

tomorrow's

GARDEN

H is for yarn–

tomorrow's

HAT

is for water–

tomorrow's

ICE CUBES

J **is for pumpkin–**

tomorrow's

JACK·O'-LANTERN

K is for tomato–

L is for bud‑

tomorrow's

LEAF

M

is for caterpillar–

tomorrow's

MOTH

N

is for twigs–

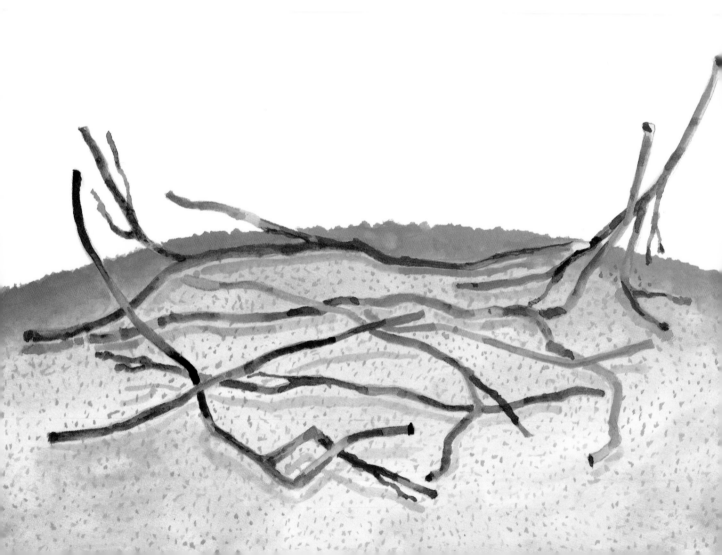

tomorrow's

NEST

O

is for acorn–

tomorrow's

OAK TREE

P **is for**
clay–

tomorrow's

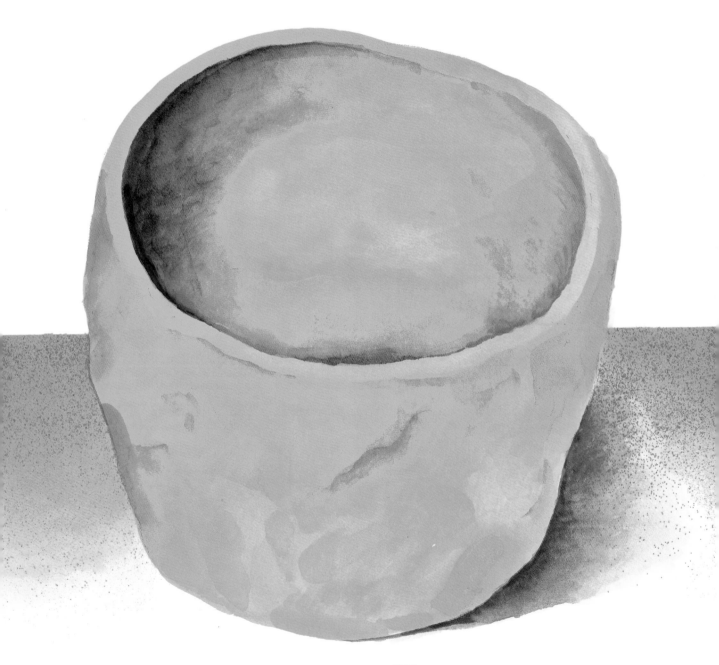

POT

Q

is for scraps–

tomorrow's

QUILT

**is for
grapes–**

tomorrow's

RAISINS

S is for vegetables–

tomorrow's

SOUP

T

is for bread–

tomorrow's

TOAST

U is for stranger–

tomorrow's

US

V is for paper–

tomorrow's

VALENTINE

W is for
stones–

tomorrow's

WALL

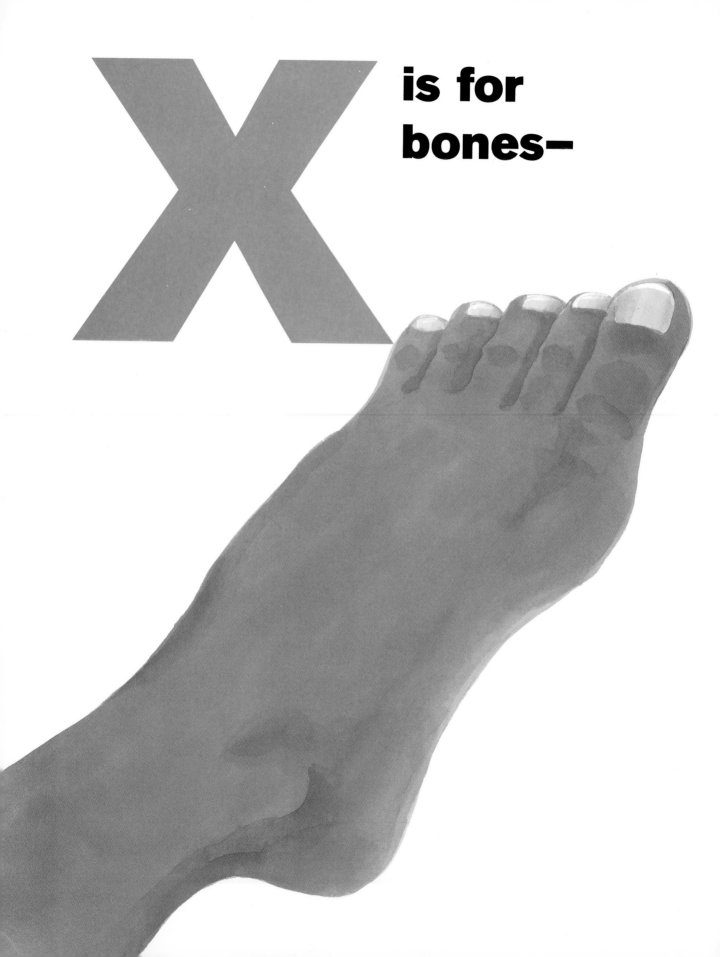

X is for bones—

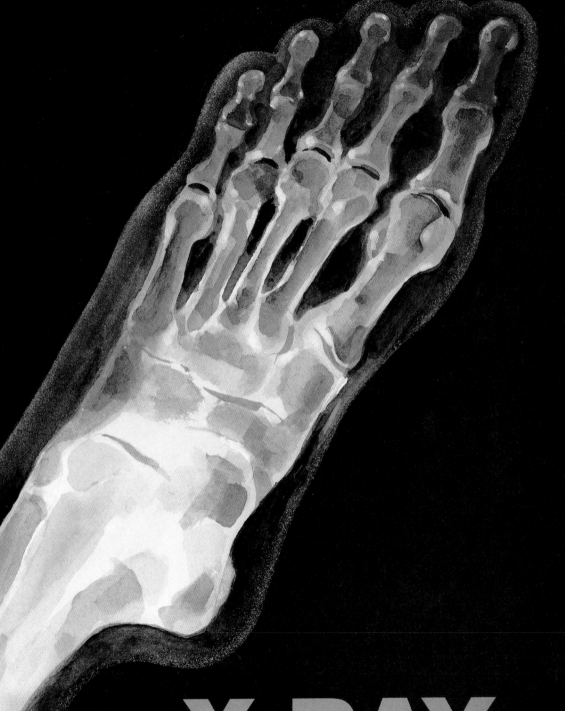

Y is for sheep–

tomorrow's

YARN

Z is for countdown—

ABCDE
FGHIJK
LMNOP
QRSTU
VWXYZ